# Get L[ost]

Written by Lesley Jane • Illustrated by Judith Trevelyan

My brother Brady
was sitting on the steps
making paper planes.

3

"Let me play.
I can make paper planes," I said.
I don't think he heard me.
"I'll play with you," said Annie.
"You are too little," I said. "Go away."
"OK," said Annie, and she did.

5

My brother Erik
was playing computer games
in his bedroom.
"I can play that computer game," I said.
I don't think he heard me.
"I'll play with you," said Annie.
"You are too silly," I said. "Get lost."
"OK," said Annie, and she did.

7

Erik and Brady
went fishing by the dam.
"I'm very good at fishing," I said.
But I don't think they heard me.
Annie looked at me.
"Get lost!" I yelled.
"OK," she said.

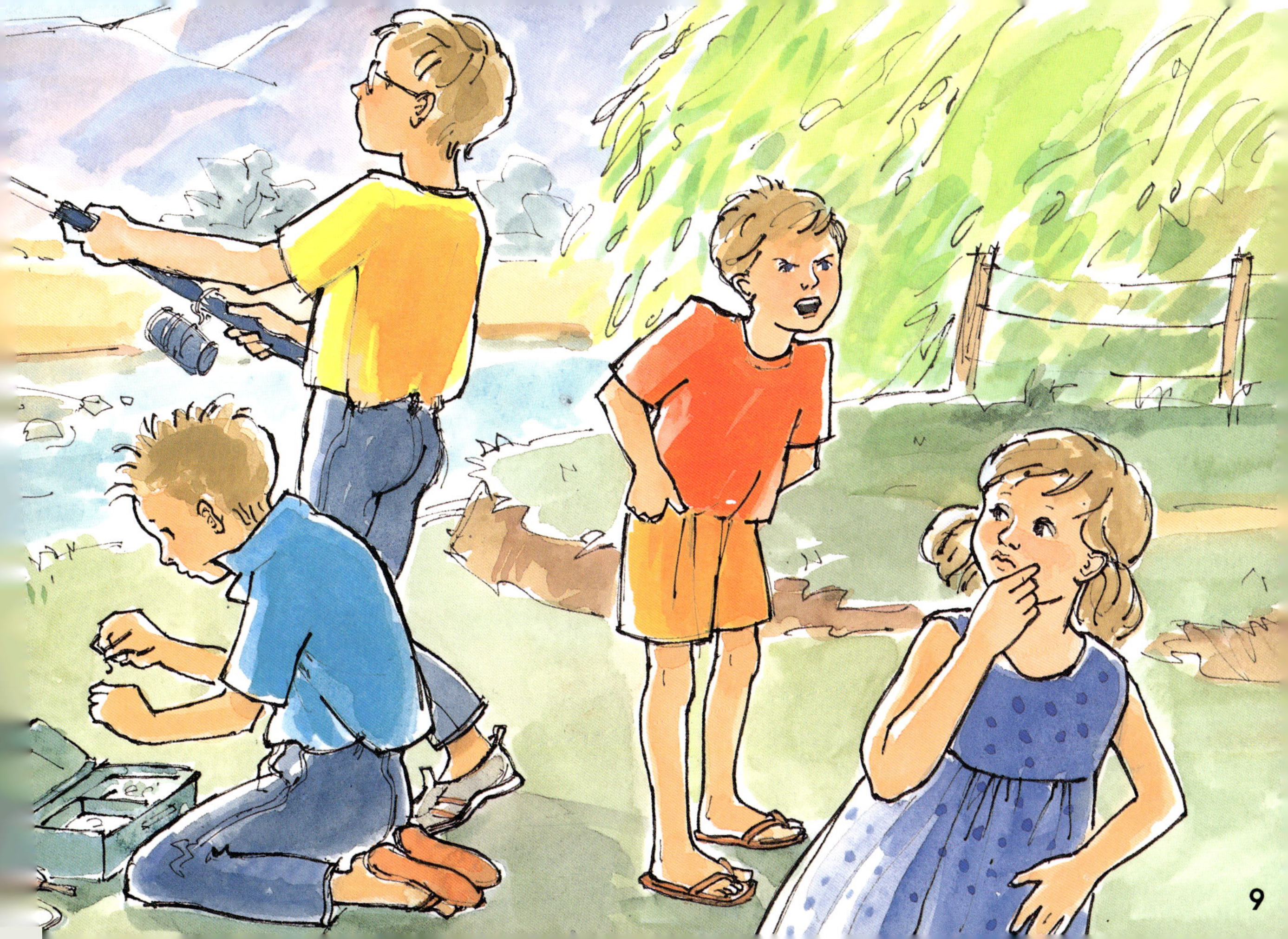

Erik and Brady
played ball in the yard.
"I can play ball.
Please let me play," I said.
"We don't want to play with you,"
said my brothers.
"GO AWAY!" they shouted, and I did.

11

I looked for Annie.
I looked everywhere.
I looked in the kitchen,
in the bedroom,
by the dam
and in the yard.

13

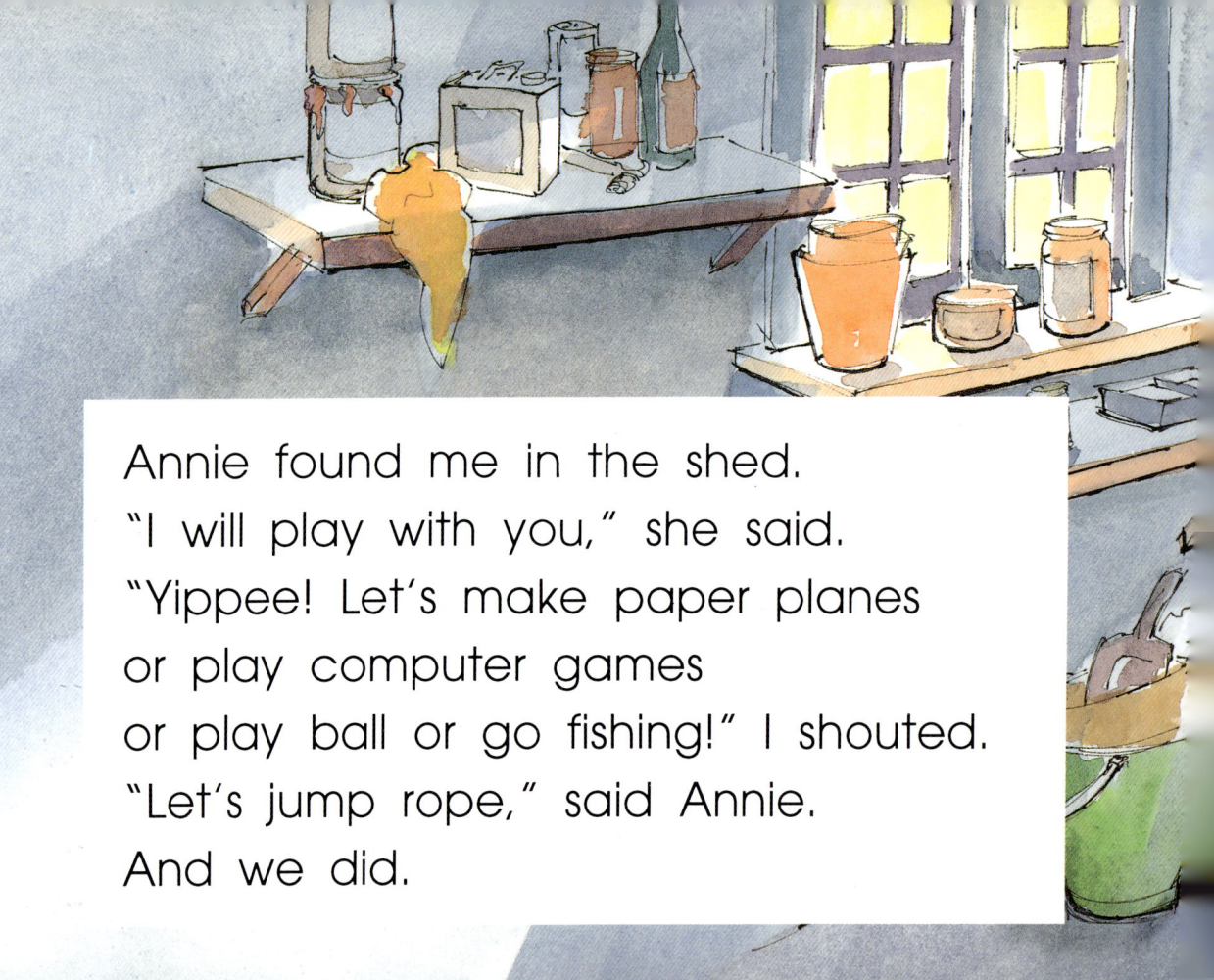

Annie found me in the shed.
"I will play with you," she said.
"Yippee! Let's make paper planes
or play computer games
or play ball or go fishing!" I shouted.
"Let's jump rope," said Annie.
And we did.

15

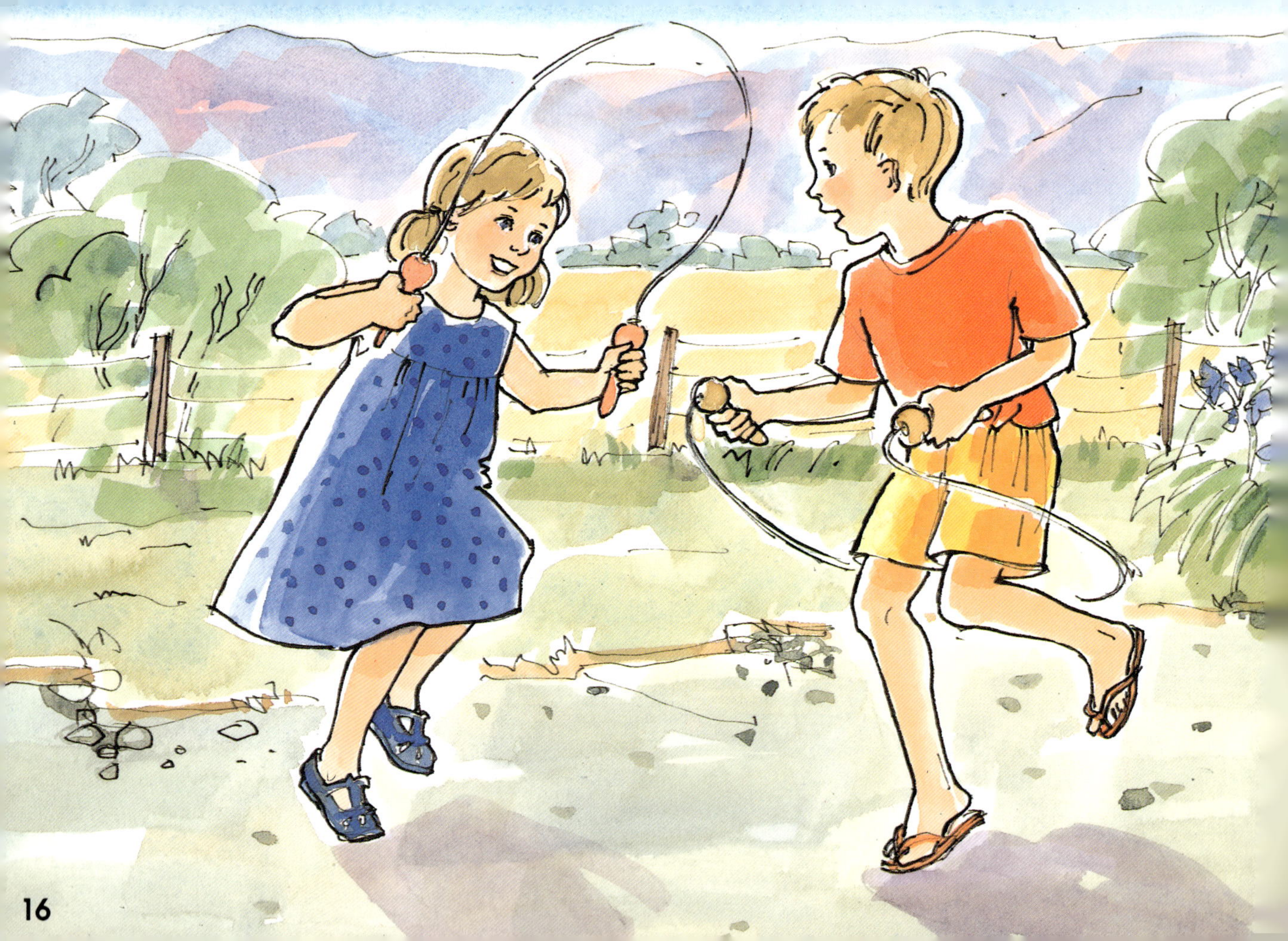